W9-BIB-113

Grammar Practice Workbook

GRADE 5

Printed in the U.S.A.

ISBN 978-0-358-24502-5

2 3 4 5 6 7 8 9 10   0928   28 27 26 25 24 23 22 21

4500821216   A B C D E F G

Grade 5 Contents

Topic 1: Sentences 1

Topic 2: Nouns, Pronouns, and Objects 21

Topic 3: Verbs 51

Topic 4: Modifiers 81

Topic 5: Conjunctions, Transitions, and Contractions 101

Topic 6: Quotations and Titles 116

Topic 7: Punctuation 126

Topic 8: Spelling 146

Review Kinds of Sentences

There are four kinds of sentences.

Declarative sentence: There are bears in the forest.
Interrogative sentence: Did you see the bear?
Imperative sentence: Do not go near the bear.
Exclamatory sentence: Watch out for the bear!

▶ **Use the words given to write a sentence. The kind of sentence is shown in parentheses. Make sure the capitalization and punctuation is correct.**

1. bears eat blueberries woods (declarative)

   _____

2. find blueberry bushes (interrogative)

   _____

3. pick berries (imperative)

   _____

4. love blueberries (exclamatory)

   _____

5. recipe blueberry pie (declarative)

   _____

▶ **Revisit a piece of your writing. Edit the draft to make sure all sentence types are written correctly.**

9

Connect to Writing: Using Different Kinds of Sentences

> **Read the selection and choose the best answer to each question.**

Kevin wrote about making movies. Read what he wrote and look for any revisions he should make. Then answer the questions that follow.

Early Movies

(1) People have been making movies since the early 1900s. (2) What was it like to make the earliest movies. (3) Watching a very old movie is exciting! (4) You can find some of them on the Internet.

(5) The earliest movies were not very complicated. (6) Don't think making those earliest movies was easy. (7) The cameras were very big and hard to move around. (8) They only recorded pictures in black and white. (9) There was no sound either, so the actors couldn't speak. (10) It is safe to say that people who made early movies had to work very hard.

1. What change, if any, should be made to Sentence 2?

    A. Change the period to an exclamation point.

    B. Change the period to a comma.

    C. Change the period to a question mark.

    D. Make no change.

2. How could you rewrite Sentence 10 to be an exclamatory sentence?

    A. The people who made the earliest movies had to work very hard!

    B. Do you think the people who made the earliest movies had to work hard?

    C. You have to work hard to make old movies.

    D. Make no change.

> **What is the oldest movie you have seen? Write two or three sentences about it.**

_____

_____

_____

_____

Complete Subjects and Predicates

Each sentence has a **complete subject** and a **complete predicate**.

A complete subject has all of the words that tell whom or what the sentence is about.

A complete predicate has all of the words that tell what the subject is or does.

complete subject	complete predicate
We all	recounted the votes.

> Circle the complete subject and underline the complete predicate in each sentence.

1. The girl with the blue ribbon was running for class president.

2. The poster with the sparkles was Reina's.

3. The past class presidents always worked to improve the school.

4. All of the students cast their votes.

5. Someone in the lobby yelled that the votes were in.

> Revisit a piece of your writing. Edit the draft to make sure complete subjects and predicates are used correctly.

Subject-Verb Agreement

> The subject and verb of a sentence should agree. Singular subjects need singular verbs. Plural subjects need plural verbs, even if a prepositional phrase stands in between the subject and verb.
>
> **plural subject and verb**   **singular subject and verb**
> We **are recounting** the votes, so everyone **has** to wait.

> ▶ **Circle the correct form of each verb.**

1. Everyone (has, have) already voted in the election. The students (is, are) excited to hear the results.

2. The principal (was, were) going to recount the votes by herself. The teachers (has, have) offered to help.

3. All of the students (think, thinks) Reina won. She (is, are) not as certain.

4. Mr. Rushing (tell, tells) the rowdy students to be patient. They (begin, begins) to quiet down.

5. The candidate with the most votes (is, are) going to win.

> ▶ **Revisit a piece of your writing. Edit the draft to make sure subject-verb agreement is used correctly.**

Compound Sentences

> In a **compound sentence**, the shorter sentences are usually joined by a comma and the word *and*, *but*, *so*, or *or*.
>
> Reina planned to write her speech alone, <u>but</u> her friends offered to help.

▷ Add the correct punctuation to make each item a compound sentence. Then write the word that is used to join the shorter sentences.

1. Blue and red confetti fell from the ceiling _____ it covered the winner.

2. Music played in the auditorium _____ we thought it was too loud.

3. The winner wanted to give a speech _____ a teacher turned down the music.

4. Reina thanked everyone for voting _____ she promised to work hard for the school.

5. She wanted to raise funds by selling class T-shirts _____ the class could wash cars.

▷ Revisit a piece of your writing. Edit the draft to make sure compound sentences are used correctly.

Review Compound Sentences

A **compound sentence** is made up of two shorter sentences joined by a comma and the **conjunction** *and*, *but*, *so*, or *or*. In each part of a compound sentence, a present-tense verb and its subject must agree in number.

▶ **Rewrite each compound sentence, using the correct punctuation and subject-verb agreement.**

1. Both candidates deserves to be class president but only one are elected.

_____

2. The principal announce the winner and the students claps.

_____

3. The winner want to talk with principal so they schedules a meeting.

_____

4. The students wants to hold a bake sale or the class could sell coupon books.

_____

5. The class president choose the fundraiser and the students is ready to help the school.

_____

Connect to Writing: Compound Sentences

> **Read the selection and choose the best answer to each question.**

*Jack wrote a paragraph about the school election. Read his paragraph
and look for any revisions he should make. Then answer the questions
that follow.*

Report on the Fifth Grade Class Election

(1) Gina has won the election! (2) Jerome was the losing candidate. (3) He was
sorry to lose. (4) He accepted his defeat. (5) Everyone celebrated Gina's victory at
Mia's house. (6) Gina gave a speech. (7) She said she was glad she won. (8) She
thanked the class for voting for her.

1. Which shows the best way to combine Sentences 3 and 4?

    A. He was sorry to lose, he accepted his defeat.

    B. He was sorry to lose, but he accepted his defeat.

    C. He was sorry to lose so he accepted his defeat.

    D. Make no change.

2. Which shows the best way to combine Sentences 7 and 8?

    A. She said she was glad she won she thanked the class for voting for her.

    B. She said she was glad she won, and she thanked the class for voting for her.

    C. She said she was glad she won or she thanked the class for voting for her.

    D. Make no change.

> **Has your class had an election? Write two or three sentences about it.**

_____

_____

_____

_____

Complex Sentences with Conjunctions

A **subordinating conjunction** connects two thoughts to make a **complex sentence**. The thought with the subordinating conjunction cannot stand on its own. It needs the rest of the sentence to make sense.

> **subordinating conjunction**
> *Because* a storm was coming, we went home early.

Some subordinating conjunctions are *if, because, when, while, since and although*.

> **Circle the subordinating conjunction in each sentence.**

1. Although it was cloudy, we decided to go for a drive.

2. We wanted to go to the beach since the weather was still warm.

3. Because it looked like it might rain, we took our umbrellas.

4. We planned to head home if the rain became too heavy.

5. While we were at the beach, we picked up some seashells.

6. When the first raindrops fell, we walked back to the car.

> **Write a sentence explaining what subordinating conjunctions do.**

_____

_____

> **Revisit a piece of your writing. Edit the draft to make sure complex sentences are used correctly.**

Dependent and Independent Clauses

A **complex sentence** is made up of a dependent clause and an independent clause. A **dependent clause** begins with a subordinating conjunction and needs the rest of the sentence to make sense. An **independent clause** can stand on its own.

    dependent clause   independent clause
When it started to rain, we went inside.

▶ **Circle the dependent clause and underline the independent clause in each sentence.**

1. We boarded up the windows because a hurricane was coming.

2. After we were finished, we went to the store for supplies.

3. Because the storm could knock down power lines, we bought flashlights.

4. We wanted to hurry back before the storm started.

5. While the hurricane raged, we stayed safe inside.

▶ **Revisit a piece of your writing. Edit the draft to make sure dependent and independent clauses are used correctly.**

Correlative Conjunctions

> **Correlative conjunctions** always work in pairs. They connect two words, phrases, or clauses that are parallel. Correlative conjunctions include *both/and, either/or, neither/nor, not only/but also, whether/or*.
>
> Not only did they make the station a museum, but they also created a special exhibit.

> ▶ **Circle the correlative conjunctions. Then underline the words, phrases, or clauses they connect.**

1. Neither the museum nor the historian could find more than one picture of the sailors.

2. Both the crew and the captain felt relieved.

> ▶ **Use the correlative conjunctions in parentheses to join the two sentences. Write the new sentence.**

1. Nathan would become a sailor depending on the outcome of his training. He would become a doctor depending on the outcome of his training. (whether/or)

_____

_____

2. Rescues were often long. They were often dangerous. (both/and)

_____

3. He was a good swimmer. He was a tremendous leader. (not only/but also)

_____

> ▶ **Revisit a piece of your writing. Edit the draft to make sure correlative conjunctions are used correctly.**

Review Complex Sentences

> A **complex sentence** contains two groups of words: an **independent clause** that can stand on its own, and a **dependent clause** that adds meaning but cannot stand on its own. The dependent clause begins with a **subordinating conjunction**, such as *when*, *because*, *if*, or *although*. These conjunctions show the relationship between the two clauses.
>
> Dave is working on his report because it is due next week.
> Because it is due next week, Dave is working on his report.

▷ Circle the subordinating conjunction in each sentence.

1. Dave found a book about women patriots while he was researching the Boston Tea Party.

2. Although women rarely took part in political protests at that time, a group of women got together in 1774 in Edenton, NC.

3. The women decided to boycott tea and other British goods because they thought the taxes were unfair.

4. When people in Britain heard about the Edenton protest, they did not take the women seriously.

▷ Underline the independent clause and circle the dependent clause in each sentence.

5. Dave will return the book to the library after he completes his project.

6. He wants to read about some of the other patriots because their stories are interesting.

7. If no other students need the book, Dave will ask the librarian if he can check it out for another week.

▷ Revisit a piece of your writing. Edit the draft to make sure complex sentences are used correctly.

Connect to Writing: Using Complex Sentences

> **Read the selection and choose the best answer to each question.**

Terry wrote a paragraph about surfing. Read his paragraph and look for any revisions he should make. Then answer the questions that follow.

Catch a Wave!

(1) Surfing can be dangerous. (2) It is a fun sport. (3) There is nothing like catching a big wave. (4) One way to start is to try body boarding. (5) A body board is a shorter surfboard that you can ride on your belly. (6) Only try it on days when the lifeguards say the ocean is safe. (7) Strong waves are dangerous. (8) A rip current could pull you out to sea.

1. Which shows the best way to combine Sentences 1 and 2?

    A. Although surfing can be dangerous, it is a fun sport.

    B. Surfing can be dangerous it is a fun sport.

    C. Because it is dangerous, surfing is a fun sport.

    D. Make no change.

2. Which shows the best way to combine sentences 7 and 8?

    A. A rip current could pull you out to sea because strong waves are dangerous.

    B. Strong waves are dangerous a rip current could pull you out to sea.

    C. Because a rip current could pull you out to sea, strong waves are dangerous.

    D. Make no change.

> **Have you tried an unusual sport? Write two or three sentences about it.**

_____

_____

_____

_____

Grade 5 • Complex Sentences

Recognizing Common and Proper Nouns

A **noun** is a word that names a person, a place, or a thing. A **common noun** names any person, place, or thing. A **proper noun** names a particular person, place, or thing.

| proper noun | common noun |

Reed Junior High School hosts the *tournament*.

> **Circle each proper noun. Underline each common noun.**

1. Francesca watches the Radio City Rockettes perform.

2. She learns dance steps from them.

3. Her dance teacher, Roma, used to be a Rockette.

4. Francesca's mother once performed at Radio City Music Hall.

> **Underline all the nouns in this paragraph.**

Sarah played with the girls on her block. The children drew hopscotch squares on the sidewalk. On Tuesday, she studied African dance at Bert's Studio.

> **Revisit a piece of your writing. Edit the draft to make sure common and proper nouns are used correctly.**

Capitalizing Proper Nouns

> **Proper nouns** must be capitalized. If a proper noun is two words, capitalize both. If it is three or more words, capitalize each important word.
>
> **proper noun**
> New York City is full of talented performers.
> Capitalize the first letter of abbreviations, such as *Mr.* or *Ms.*, and end with a period.
> Also capitalize initials, such as *C. S. Lewis*, and acronyms, such as *FBI*.

> **Write the sentence on the line. Capitalize the proper nouns.**

1. The jump rope team from harlem is very talented.

   _____

2. Their team name is dazzling ropers.

   _____

3. They performed at the thanksgiving day parade in new york.

   _____

> **Write the sentence on the line. Capitalize abbreviations, initials, and acronyms.**

4. My mother jumped rope on the corner of 125th st and second ave in nyc.

   _____

5. mr david a. walker developed double dutch into a world class sport.

   _____

> **Revisit a piece of your writing. Edit the draft to make sure proper nouns are capitalized correctly.**

Capitalizing Organizations

When a proper noun is the name of an organization, capitalize each important word. An acronym is a proper noun made up of initials, or the first letter of important words. Capitalize all of the letters in an acronym.

name of organization	acronym
University of North Texas	UNT

> Rewrite each sentence on the line below it. Capitalize the proper nouns.

1. Would you like to see jumping rope as a sport in the olympics?

   _____

2. The team from Japan is one of the best in the international double dutch federation.

   _____

3. talura reid invented her rope-turning machine at the university of michigan.

   _____

4. The american double dutch league is also called addl.

   _____

5. dddd stands for a group called dynamic diplomats of double dutch.

   _____

> Revisit a piece of your writing. Edit the draft to make sure organizations are capitalized correctly.

Review Common and Proper Nouns

A **common noun** is the name of a person, place, or thing. **A proper noun** is the name of a particular person, place, or thing. A proper noun always begins with a capital letter.

> Circle the common noun in each sentence. Underline any proper nouns.

1. The lighthouse is located in North Carolina.

2. Herbert Greenley built it to help sailors.

3. It helps them see during strong storms.

4. Greenley was proud of the building he created.

> Correct six errors in this paragraph. Circle the errors and write the words correctly on the lines below.

The lusitania was the name of a ship. It was built in great Britain over a hundred years ago and made several trips across the atlantic. In 1915, it was hit with torpedoes from a Submarine. At the time, Britain was in a War with germany. Eighteen minutes after it was struck, the ship sank.

5. _____

6. _____

7. _____

8. _____

9. _____

10. _____

> Revisit a piece of your writing. Edit the draft to make sure common and proper nouns are used correctly.

Connect to Writing: Using Common and Proper Nouns

> **Read the selection and choose the best answer to each question.**

*Mariko wrote a paragraph about baseball. Read her paragraph and look for
any revisions she should make. Then answer the questions that follow.*

Baseball in Japan

(1) Two years ago, my Dad left his job with major league baseball to work for
Nippon professional baseball, which is like a Japanese mlb. (2) My family moved to
Tokyo in April, when the Japanese school year begins. (3) I was worried about being
the Newcomer at Tokyo Girls' Middle School. (4) Then I found out that everyone
loved to jump rope during recess. (5) Some girls, like etsuko and tomoko, can do
stunts and tricks.

1. Which of the following ways could you rewrite Sentence 1?

   A. Two years ago, my dad left his job with Major League Baseball to work for
   Nippon professional baseball, which is like a Japanese mlb.

   B. Two years ago, my dad left his job with Major League Baseball to work for
   Nippon Professional Baseball, which is like a Japanese MLB.

   C. Two years ago, my Dad left his job with Major League Baseball to work for
   Nippon professional baseball, which is like a Japanese MLB.

   D. Make no change.

2. What change, if any, should be made to Sentence 5?

   A. Capitalize Etsuko and Tomoko.

   B. Capitalize Girls.

   C. Capitalize Stunts and Tricks.

   D. Make no change.

> **What is your favorite sport? Write two or three sentences about it.**

_____

_____

_____

_____

Plural Nouns

A **singular noun** names one person, place, thing, or idea. A **plural noun** names more than one person, place, thing, or idea. Form the plural of most nouns by adding *-s* or *-es*. Look at the ending of a singular noun to decide how to form the plural.

We celebrated a lot of <u>holidays</u> in Mexico.

▶ **Write the plural form of the noun in parentheses.**

1. During May we had (celebration) on Cinco de Mayo. _____

2. It is the day the Mexican army defeated (soldier) from France. _____

3. People in the government give (speech) and everyone plays (game). _____

4. Many people have (party) during the day and eat Mexican (dish). _____

5. People dance to Mexican (song) and wear Mexican (costume). _____

▶ **Revisit a piece of your writing. Edit the draft to make sure singular and plural nouns are used correctly.**

Name _____

Irregular Plurals

Many nouns are not made plural according to the regular rules. To form the plural of some nouns ending in *f* or *fe*, change the *f* to *v* and add *-es*. For others, add *-s*. To form the plural of nouns ending in *o*, add *-s* or *-es*. Some nouns have the same form whether singular or plural.

My grandfather has two <u>shelves</u> of books about our culture.

> **Write the plural form of the noun in parentheses.**

1. Preparing our family's Thanksgiving dinner takes two (day). _____

2. Some of the (woman) search the woods for wild berries. _____

3. Sometimes they see (goose) overhead while walking home. _____

4. My father always divides the pumpkin pies in two (half). _____

5. Every year we say that it is the best meal of our (life). _____

> **Revisit a piece of your writing. Edit the draft to make sure irregular plural nouns are used correctly.**

Collective Nouns

A **collective noun** names a group of people, animals, or things that act as a unit. Treat a collective noun like a singular noun, unless it names more than one group.

> **singular collective noun**
> Our <u>class</u> planned a celebration.
>
> **plural collective noun**
> All grade 5 <u>classes</u> are invited.

▶ **Underline the collective noun in each sentence. Write whether each collective noun is singular or plural.**

1. The teacher chose Elisa for the spelling team. _____

2. José spoke to a school audience about the traditions of Guatemala. _____

3. Anila's father is on several committees at the community center. _____

4. In the United States, a jury decides whether a person is innocent or guilty

   of a crime. _____

5. Both groups planned to perform a show together in August. _____

▶ **Revisit a piece of your writing. Edit the draft to make sure collective nouns are used correctly.**

Review Singular and Plural Nouns

> A noun that names only one person, place, or thing is a **singular noun**. A noun that names more than one person, place, or thing is a **plural noun**. Most plural nouns are formed by adding -*s* or -*es*. Some are formed in other ways and need to be memorized. A **collective noun** names a group of people, animals, or things that act as a unit. A collective noun is treated as a singular noun, unless it names more than one group or collection.

▶ **Write the underlined singular noun as a plural noun.**

1. Dora's <u>teammate</u> were great at basketball. _____

2. They played both <u>half</u> of the game well. _____

3. Basketballs were kept on <u>shelf</u> in the storage closet. _____

4. The players wore mouthguards to protect their <u>tooth</u>. _____

5. The <u>lady</u> who live near school come to every game. _____

▶ **Revisit a piece of your writing. Edit the draft to make sure singular and plural nouns are used correctly.**

Connect to Writing: Singular and Plural Nouns

> **Read the selection and choose the best answer to each question.**

Ryan wrote a paragraph about football practice. Read his paragraph and look for any revisions he should make. Then answer the questions that follow.

Football Practice

(1) Coach blew the whistle to get our attention. (2) Billy was still tying his new things. (3) Coach told a joke that made everyone laugh. (4) We were nervous about the upcoming game. (5) We played well in practice. (6) After, Coach took us to the place for food.

1. Which of the following ways could you rewrite Sentence 2 to use a more precise noun?

   A. Billy was still tying his new cleats.

   B. Billy was still doing something with his new things.

   C. Billy was still tying his shoes.

   D. Make no change.

2. What change, if any, should be made to Sentence 6?

   A. Change *Coach* to *the man*.

   B. Change *us* to *people*.

   C. Change *place for food* to *pizza restaurant*.

   D. Make no change.

> **What do you like to do after school? Write two or three sentences about it.**

_____

_____

_____

_____

Singular Possessive Nouns

A singular possessive noun shows that one person, place, or thing has or owns something. To show a singular possessive noun, add an apostrophe and -s ('s) to a singular noun.

Singular Noun
the ear of the elephant

Singular Possessive Noun
the elephant's ear

> Each underlined phrase can be rewritten in a shorter way. Rewrite each sentence, using a possessive noun.

1. The research of Dr. Payne proved that elephants can hear noises that humans can't.

_____

2. The insect will become the dinner of the hungry bat.

_____

3. The dance the bee does shows the other honeybees where to find pollen.

_____

4. In order to track its movements, the scientist put a band around the leg of the bird.

_____

5. Many animals use the magnetic field of Earth to navigate over long distances.

_____

> Revisit a piece of your writing. Edit the draft to make sure singular possessive nouns are used correctly.

Plural Possessive Nouns

A **plural possessive noun** shows that more than one person, place, or thing has or owns something.

- When a plural noun ends in -s, add only an apostrophe after the -s (s').
- When a plural noun does not end in -s, add ('s) to form the plural possessive noun

Plural Noun

the hive of the *bees*   the den of the *mice*

Plural Possessive Noun

the bees' hive   the mice's den

> **Each underlined phrase can be rewritten in a shorter way. Rewrite each sentence, adding plural possessive nouns.**

1. Scientists continue to study senses of animals.

   _____

2. We could hear the trumpeting calls of the elephants from a long distance.

   _____

3. The decline of several species of trout is being noticed in local streams.

   _____

4. Bats use echoes to find the location of their prey.

   _____

5. I read about how bees dance in a science article for children.

   _____

> **Revisit a piece of your writing. Edit the draft to make sure plural possessive nouns are used correctly.**

Using Possessive Nouns

A **singular possessive noun** shows ownership for one person, place, or thing. To show a singular possessive noun, add an apostrophe and -*s* to a singular noun.

A **plural possessive noun** shows ownership for more than one person, place, or thing. When a plural noun ends in -*s*, add only an apostrophe after the -*s* (*s'*). When a plural noun does not end in -*s*, add an apostrophe and an -*s* (*'s*).

Noun

fur of the dog   dishes of the dogs   the club of women

Possessive Noun

dog's fur   dogs' dishes   the women's club

> **Each underlined phrase can be written in a shorter way. Rewrite each sentence, adding plural possessive nouns.**

1. The <u>constant eating of the hungry mice</u> ruined the wheat crop.

   _____

2. The hunter woke up to the thunder of <u>the hooves of the stampeding deer.</u>

   _____

3. Depending on <u>the strength of the oxen,</u> the farmer filled his wagon with cotton bales.

   _____

4. The <u>offspring of snow geese</u> spend their first months on the Arctic tundra.

   _____

5. Migrating zebras aroused the <u>interest of the children.</u>

   _____

> **Revisit a piece of your writing. Edit the draft to make sure possessive nouns are used correctly.**

33

Review Possessive Nouns

Singular Noun	Singular Possessive	Plural Noun	Plural Possessive
Carla	Carla's hat	buckets	buckets' handles
book	book's chapters	people	people's ideas

> **Write the possessive form of the noun in parentheses.**

1. (students) The _____ mouths were opened in shock.

2. (box) They could not believe the _____ contents.

3. (Today) _____ activity is examining plants.

4. (Sam) _____ stomach ached from laughing so hard.

> **Combine the sentences using possessive nouns. Write the new sentence on the line.**

5. The students were using computers. The computers belonged to the school.

   _____

6. The coughing disturbed the students and their two teachers. The principal was coughing.

   _____

7. The robots rushed toward the door. The robots belonged to the teachers.

   _____

> **Revisit a piece of your writing. Edit the draft to make sure possessive nouns are used correctly.**

Connect to Writing: Using Possessive Nouns

> Read the selection and choose the best answer to each question.

*Aaron wrote a paragraph about a trip he took. Read his paragraph and
look for any revisions he should make. Then answer the questions that follow.*

Salmon Fishing

(1) My uncle has a cabin. (2) It is near the place where the river meets the sea.
(3) Salmon breed in the river. (4) It is a good place to go fishing. (5) Uncle Steve has a
boat. (6) We will use it to catch fish. (7) I have a red and silver fishing lure that is
great for catching salmon. (8) We will cook fish for dinner after we catch it!

1. Which of the following ways could you rewrite Sentences 1 and 2 to combine them?

    A. My uncle has a cabin it is near where the river meets the sea.

    B. My uncle's cabin is near the place where the river meets the sea.

    C. My uncles cabin it is near where the river meets the sea.

    D. Make no change.

2. Which of the following ways could you rewrite Sentences 5 and 6 to combine them?

    A. Uncle Steve has a boat we will use it to catch fish.

    B. Uncle Steve's boat catches fish.

    C. We will use Uncle Steve's boat to catch fish.

    D. Make no change.

> What is something interesting you did on vacation? Write two or three sentences about it.

_____

_____

_____

_____

Subject Pronouns

A **pronoun** is a word that takes the place of a noun. A **subject pronoun** performs the action of the verb in a sentence.

singular subject pronouns: I, you, he, she, it
plural subject pronouns: we, you, they

Jane read her history text.   She read her history test.
Ed and Mark studied for the test.   They studied for the test.

> **Underline the subject in each sentence. Replace the noun(s) with a subject pronoun.**

1. Ken, Lee, and Martha want to write a play about the Revolutionary War. _____

2. Martha begins researching the topic. _____

3. The play takes many weeks to plan. _____

4. Harry builds the set for the play. _____

5. The story focuses on the ride of Paul Revere. _____

> **Underline the correct subject pronoun(s) in each sentence.**

6. (They, Them) are changing the rehearsal schedule.

7. (We, You) would like to hear your opinion.

8. (You, I) were just voted director of the play.

9. Mark and (me, I) will make the costumes.

10. However, (he, him) and (I, me) will ask others to help.

> **Revisit a piece of your writing. Edit the draft to make sure subject pronouns are used correctly.**

Object Pronouns

A **pronoun** is a word that takes the place of a noun. An **object pronoun** takes the place of a noun used after an action verb or after a word such as *to, for, with, in,* or *out*.

singular object pronouns: me, you, him, her, it
plural object pronouns: us, you, them

History is easy for <u>Liam</u>. History is easy for <u>him</u>.
Lars went with <u>Mike and Aiden</u>. Lars went with <u>them</u>.

> Read each sentence pair. Put an X on the blank by the sentence with the correct object pronoun.

1. _____ Ken wanted me to play Paul Revere.

   _____ Ken wanted I to play Paul Revere.

2. _____ He offered parts in the play to he and she.

   _____ He offered parts in the play to him and her.

3. _____ Martha emailed copies of the script to we.

   _____ Martha emailed copies of the script to us.

4. _____ It was a good way for them to study history.

   _____ It was a good way for they to study history.

5. _____ My parents applauded loudly for I.

   _____ My parents applauded loudly for me.

> Revisit a piece of your writing. Edit the draft to make sure object pronouns are used correctly.

Pronoun-Antecedent Agreement

A **pronoun** is a word that takes the place of a noun. An **antecedent** is the word the pronoun replaces or refers to. A pronoun and its antecedent must agree in number and gender.

pronoun	sentence	antecedent
I	I am Emily.	Emily
you	You are Jana.	Jana
he	He is Jarrod.	Jarrod
she	My dog barks when she plays.	dog
they	My dogs rest after they exercise.	dogs

▸ **Underline the pronoun and circle the antecedent in each.**

1. Joshua said he would dim the lights from backstage.

2. Mary turned on the flashlight, but it did not work.

3. Lucy hoped she had extra batteries in her pocket.

4. Andy's friends helped him practice his lines for the play.

5. The class shouted, "We are going to be great tonight!"

▸ **Revisit a piece of your writing. Edit the draft to make sure pronoun-antecedent agreement is used correctly.**

Review Subject and Object Pronouns

Nouns	Subject Pronouns
Brian and Beth go to the bookstore. The one who wants a book is Brian.	They go to the bookstore. He wants a book.
Nouns	**Object Pronouns**
Brian bought this book. Brian gave these books to Chris and Anthony.	Brian bought it. Brian gave these books to them.

> Circle the correct pronoun in parentheses. Then label the pronoun subject or object.

1. Have (you, her) ever read a comic book? _____

2. (He/Him) reads many comic books. _____

3. Kathy listens to (him, he) talk about comic books. _____

4. When a new comic is released, Roger is the first to buy (it, them). _____

5. Roger buys an extra copy for (I, me). _____

6. (I, Me) thank Roger! _____

> Circle four errors in the paragraph and write corrections on the line below. Subject and object pronouns are misused.

In my favorite comic book, the images help show the characters' superpowers. One of they can control the weather with her mind! Another character can walk through walls. Him is my favorite character. When I create a comic book someday, I will include a character like he. In my comic book, all the superheroes will be able to fly to the planets in outer space in seconds. My sister can draw and paint really well. I guess her and I can work together, but only if she remembers that I am the boss!

_____

> Revisit a piece of your writing. Edit the draft to make sure subject and object pronouns are used correctly.

_____

Connect to Writing: Using Subject and Object Pronouns

> **Connect to Writing: Using Subject and Object Pronouns**

Rayna wrote a paragraph about something that happened at school. Read her paragraph and look for any revisions she should make. Then answer the questions that follow.

The History Test

(1) Kara was late to class. (2) The test had already started when Kara arrived. (3) The test was about John Adams and Thomas Jefferson. (4) Will and Matt were nervous about how Will and Matt would do on the test. (5) Will was the first one to turn in the test to the teacher. (6) Kara worried she would fail the test and Kara was the last one to finish.

1. Which of the following ways could you rewrite Sentence 4?

   A. Will and Matt were nervous about how Matt and Will would do on the test.

   B. Will and Matt were nervous about how they would do on the test.

   C. They were nervous about how them would do on the test.

   D. Make no change.

2. What change, if any, should be made to Sentence 6?

   A. Change the second Kara *to she.*

   B. Change *she* to *Kara.*

   C. Change *test* to *it.*

   D. Make no change.

> **How do you feel right before you take a test? Write two or three sentences about it.**

_____

_____

_____

_____

Indefinite Pronouns

An **indefinite pronoun** takes the place of a noun. It can stand for a person, place, or thing. The noun that it stands for is unclear or not identified.

indefinite pronoun
<u>Someone</u> wrote a letter to the city council.

> **Circle the correct pronoun that completes each sentence.**

1. (All, Every) of us wanted to go swimming this summer.

2. However, (someone, something) decided to close the city pool.

3. We asked if (nobody, anyone) on the city council could reopen the pool.

4. The council members said there was (everything, nothing) they could do.

5. We decided to search for (someone, somewhere) else to go swimming.

> **Revisit a piece of your writing. Edit the draft to make sure indefinite pronouns are used correctly.**

Possessive Pronouns

A **possessive pronoun** shows ownership. Possessive pronouns like *mine*, *yours*, *its*, and *ours* can stand alone and take the place of a noun. Other possessive pronouns such as *my*, *your*, *its*, and *our* come before a noun.

> **possessive pronouns**
> The speech was <u>his</u> and not <u>hers</u>.
> <u>My</u> friends came to the meeting.

> **Underline the possessive pronouns.**

1. Shepherd's pie is our favorite dinner.

2. Those plates and cups are ours.

3. This seat is yours if you want to join us.

4. Alice brought her sister.

5. I know this bag is mine because its zipper is broken.

> **Revisit a piece of your writing. Edit the draft to make sure possessive pronouns are used correctly.**

Interrogative Pronouns

An **interrogative pronoun** replaces a person, place, or thing in a question. Some interrogative pronouns are *who*, *what*, and *which*.

interrogative pronouns
<u>Who</u> wanted to start a community garden?

> **Write an interrogative pronoun to complete each question.**

1. _____ planted the flowers in the garden?

2. _____ does she grow there?

3. _____ of these flowers does she like most?

4. _____ does she plan to grow next?

5. _____ would like to help me start a vegetable garden?

> **Revisit a piece of your writing. Edit the draft to make sure interrogative pronouns are used correctly.**

Review Pronouns

A **pronoun** is a word that takes the place of a noun. There are several kinds of pronouns. Words such as *someone* and *something* refer to a person or thing that is not identified. These pronouns are called **indefinite pronouns**. Pronouns that replace possessive nouns are called **possessive pronouns**. Words such as *who*, *what*, and *which* can be used to begin questions. These pronouns are called **interrogative pronouns**.

> Underline the indefinite pronoun, possessive pronoun, or interrogative pronoun in each sentence. Write the type of pronoun on the line.

1. Who is the woman in the purple dress? _____

2. Everyone asks the gardener about flowers. _____

3. Her flowers are larger and more colorful than the rest. _____

4. Which is garden is Mrs. Johnson's? _____

5. The garden on Mott Street is hers. _____

> Revisit a piece of your writing. Edit the draft to make sure pronouns are used correctly.

Connect to Writing: Using Indefinite, Possessive, and Interrogative Pronouns

> Read the selection and choose the best answer to each question.

Samantha wrote a paragraph about a speech she saw. Read her paragraph and look for any revisions she should make. Then answer the questions that follow.

How Can You Help?

(1) I read an article about homeless people by Mina Lawson. (2) I went to see her speak at the community center. (3) I listened to the mayor's speech and then to her speech. (4) Mrs. Lawson discussed how the community can help the homeless. (5) Today is my turn to help Mrs. Lawson, and tomorrow it's your turn to help.

1. Which of the following ways could you rewrite Sentence 3 to avoid repeated nouns?

   A. I listened to the mayor's speech and then to hers.

   B. I listened to the mayor's speech and Mrs. Lawson's speech.

   C. I listened to the mayor's speech and, after the mayor, Mrs. Lawson's speech.

   D. Make no change.

2. Which of the following ways could you rewrite Sentence 5 to avoid repeated nouns?

   A. Today and tomorrow is my and your turn to help Mrs. Lawson.

   B. Today is my turn to help, and tomorrow is your turn to help.

   C. Today is my turn to help Mrs. Lawson, and tomorrow it's yours.

   D. Make no change.

> Write two or three sentences about a cause that you feel strongly about.

_____

_____

_____

_____

Direct Objects

In a sentence, a **direct object** is a person, place, or thing that receives the action of the verb. The direct object can be either a noun or a pronoun (it, someone, him).

The dog loved the <u>boy</u>.

> Underline the direct object in each sentence.

1. Papa is herding cattle.

2. Mama will fix the fence.

3. I will plant seeds.

4. Last month, a mountain lion attacked our neighbors' cow.

5. Their hired man saw it.

6. He scared it away.

7. That story frightened me.

8. Our parents warned us to stay on the ranch.

9. I will never forget the bear we met in the woods.

10. After that time, we paid attention.

> Revisit a piece of your writing. Edit the draft to make sure direct objects are used correctly.

Compound Direct Objects

A **compound direct** object is two or more objects that
receive the action of the same verb. The objects can be
nouns, pronouns, or both. The object forms of personal
pronouns are *me, you, her, him, it, us, you, them*.

Mama called <u>Papa, the hired man, and my brother</u>.
Mama called <u>my brother and me</u>.

> In each sentence, underline the compound direct object.

1. I gathered a hammer, nails, and glue.

2. I fixed the fence, the barn, and the front door.

3. We welcomed our neighbors and some traveling musicians.

4. The musicians entertained our neighbors and us.

> Underline the incorrect object pronouns. Write the correct ones.

5. The moon and stars helped they and us see better. _____

6. Papa says the darkness never scared Mama or he. _____

7. Still, you won't find my brother or I out after dark. _____

> Revisit a piece of your writing. Edit the draft to make sure compound direct objects
are used correctly.

Indirect Objects

An **indirect object** is a noun or a pronoun that comes between the verb and the direct object. An indirect object tells to or for whom or what the action of the verb is done. A sentence that has an indirect object must have a direct object.

    indirect object   direct object
    Papa gave his <u>horse</u> a **pat** on the head.

> Underline the indirect object and draw two lines under the direct object.

1. Our cousins showed us the swimming hole on their ranch.

2. They handed us fishing poles.

3. We brought the ducks and geese small pieces of bread.

4. We took the cows and horses their feed.

5. They got her a snack.

> Revisit a piece of your writing. Edit the draft to make sure direct and indirect objects are used correctly.

Review Direct and Indirect Objects

A **direct object** is a person, place, or thing that receives the action of a verb.

An **indirect object** is a noun or a pronoun that comes between the verb and the direct object. An indirect object tells to or for whom or what the action of the verb is done.

▶ **The action verb in each sentence is printed in bold type. Find the direct object and circle it. Then underline the indirect object, if one is used.**

1. I **wrote** Amy a letter.

2. She **described** the eclipse.

3. I **gave** our dog a treat.

4. Amy **mailed** me a pen.

5. I **wrote** Mom and Dad using the pen.

▶ **Revisit a piece of your writing. Edit the draft to make sure direct and indirect objects are used correctly.**

Connect to Writing: Using Direct and Indirect Objects

▶ **Read the selection and choose the best answer to each question.**

Mary wrote a paragraph imagining she lived in a historical period. Read her paragraph and look for any revisions she should make. Then answer the questions that follow.

On the Farm

(1) Papa rode the big red stallion. (2) Papa rode the palomino. (3) Mama made quilts for our beds. (4) When we rode in the wagon, we saw deer running. (5) We saw hawks circling. (6) We have chicken for supper. (7) We are safe from dangerous wildlife inside.

1. Which shows the best way to combine Sentences 1 and 2?

   A. The big red stallion and the palomino Papa rode.

   B. Papa rode the big red stallion Papa rode the palomino.

   C. Papa road the big red stallion and the palomino.

   D. Make no change.

2. Which shows the best way to combine Sentences 4 and 5?

   A. When we rode in the wagon, we saw deer running and hawks circling.

   B. When we rode in the wagon, we saw deer running we saw hawks circling

   C. When we rode in the wagon we saw deer running and we saw hawks circling.

   D. Make no change.

▶ **What do you think it would be like to live in the past? Write two or three sentences about it.**

_____

_____

_____

_____

Linking and Action Verbs

An **action verb** shows what the subject does or did.

action verb
↓
The koala climbed the tree.

A **linking verb** connects the subject of the sentence to the predicate or the object.

linking verb
↓
Koalas are small and furry animals.

> **Underline the action verb in each sentence.**

1. I studied about the animals.

2. The scientists searched the forest for koalas.

3. The team marched through the forest.

4. We followed the old path.

5. The team boarded a plane for home.

> **Underline the linking verb in each sentence.**

6. Koalas are herbivores.

7. These animals look like little bears.

8. The koala is a wild animal.

9. We felt tired after the long hike.

10. The koala's fur was gray and white.

> **Revisit a piece of your writing. Edit the draft to make sure all linking and action verbs are used correctly.**

Main and Helping Verbs

A **main verb** tells what the subject is thinking or doing. A
helping verb comes before the main verb and adds detail.
Some helping verbs are *may*, *might*, *must*, *been*, *is*, *do*,
should, *have*, *will*, and *can*.

helping verb main verb
↓   ↓
We <u>may</u> <u>go</u> to the rainforest soon.

▶ **Underline the main verb of each sentence once. Then underline the helping verb of
each sentence twice.**

1. I would love to see a tree kangaroo.

2. We will study the animals of Papua New Guinea in class.

3. We have learned about forest habitats.

4. The biologist will share the findings of the study.

5. The tree kangaroos can return to their home in the trees.

6. The workers have located two tree kangaroos.

7. I would enjoy the presentation very much.

8. I have seen a program about those animals on TV.

9. We have tried many different programs.

10. The show about kangaroos may be my favorite.

▶ **Revisit a piece of your writing. Edit the draft to make sure all main and helping verbs
are used correctly.**

Verb Tenses

> **Verb tense** can help convey times, sequences, conditions, or states. The verbs in the sentence below convey a sequence of events.
>
> After the scientists <u>have found</u> a koala, they <u>will examine</u> it.

▶ **For each of the following sentences, identify whether the verb tenses are helping to convey time, sequence, condition, or state.**

1. We walk through the forest in search of koalas. _____

2. We flew to Australia and will drive to the camp. _____

3. The men had to capture the animal before examining it. _____

4. We will have completed a full week's worth of work in the forest. _____

5. I will be delighted to be done with this project. _____

6. We will be flying to a remote part of the continent. _____

7. I followed the animal I spotted in the trees. _____

8. The koalas will recover if they are given enough time. _____

9. They will tell us when we can return to the forest. _____

10. We will set up a tent on the first day. _____

▶ **Revisit a piece of your writing. Edit the draft to make sure all verb tenses are used correctly.**

Review Verbs

> **Time:** conveys past, present, or future
> The cougar <u>crept</u> into its lair. (*action verb*)
> **Sequence:** conveys order of events
> <u>Read</u> the book, and then we <u>will discuss</u> cougars. (*action verb; helping verb*)
> **Condition:** conveys that one action or state of being depends on a condition
> being met
> If the trackers <u>catch</u> a cougar, they <u>will tag</u> it. (*action verb; helping verb*)
> **State:** conveys a subject's state of being
> The cougar <u>felt</u> frightened without its mother. (*linking verb*)

▶ **On the line following each sentence, tell if the verb or verbs express time, sequence, condition, or state.**

1. The cubs greedily drank the milk. _____

2. After they play, they will eat again. _____

3. If they go to the watering hole, they may fall in. _____

4. The mother cougar watches their moves carefully. _____

5. She feels anxious about their safety. _____

▶ **Write one paragraph about cougars that shows verb tenses used to convey time, sequence, condition, and state.**

_____

_____

_____

_____

_____

▶ **Revisit a piece of your writing. Edit the draft to make sure all verb tenses are used correctly.**

_____

Connect to Writing: Using Linking and Action Verbs

> **Read the selection and choose the best answer to each question.**

Mario wrote a paragraph about a kangaroo. Read his paragraph and look for any revisions he should make. Then answer the questions that follow.

A Trip to Australia

(1) When I was in Australia, I saw a kangaroo. (2) The kangaroo is a strange animal. (3) Mama kangaroos have babies called joeys. (4) They have joeys in a pouch. (5) Kangaroos also have powerful legs for hopping. (6) A kangaroo goes surprisingly fast!

1. Which of the following ways could you rewrite Sentence 4 to include a more precise verb?

   A. They get joeys in a pouch.

   B. They carry joeys in a pouch.

   C. They are joeys in a pouch.

   D. Make no change.

2. What change, if any, should be made to Sentence 6 to add a more precise verb?

   A. Change *fast* to *faster*.

   B. Chang *goes* to *is*.

   C. Change *goes* to *jumps*.

   D. Make no change.

> **What exciting adventure have you had? Write two or three sentences about it.**

_____

_____

_____

_____

Present and Past Tense

The **tense** of a verb shows the time of an action or event. Verbs in **present tense** show that an event is happening now or regularly. Verbs in **past tense** show that an event has already happened. To form the past tense of most verbs, you can add *-d* or *-ed*.

present tense
↓
Today, most Americans <u>live</u> in or near cities.

past tense
↓
Most of the American colonists <u>lived</u> on farms.

> **Write the verbs in each sentence and tell whether they are in present or past tense.**

1. Pedro shared how the New England colonists lived.

   _____

2. During the summer break, he travels to Virginia and visits a living history museum.

   _____

3. He bought a bottle that a glassblower created from melted sand.

   _____

4. Pedro's little sister traveled with him, and she still remembers the trip.

   _____

5. They both decided that the furniture in the houses seemed tiny.

   _____

> **Revisit a piece of your writing. Edit the draft to make sure all present- and past-tense verbs are used correctly.**

Future Tense

Verbs in **future tense** show that an event is going to happen. To form the future tense, use a helping verb such as *will*.

present tense
↓
She <u>learns</u> about American history.

future tense
↓
She <u>will learn</u> about American history.

To shorten a future-tense verb, you can use a contraction.
<u>She will learn</u> contracts to <u>she'll learn</u>.

> Write the future tense of the verb in parentheses. Write both the full future tense and the contraction.

1. She (takes) a field trip with her class. _____

2. They (visit) the site of a famous battle. _____

3. She (sees) the bridge that she read about in school. _____

4. They (talk) to the park ranger about the battle. _____

5. The teacher calculates how much it (costs) to buy copies of a historic map for their classroom. _____

> Revisit a piece of your writing. Edit the draft to make sure all future-tense verbs are used correctly.

Name _____

Consistent Use of Tenses

Verb tenses help readers understand when different events in a story happen. To clearly show when events take place, choose the best tense for the situation. Change the tense only when you want to show a change in time.

Yesterday, we **started** to research our history project. Today, we **make** a poster for the presentations. We **will complete** the project next week.

> Read the sentences and think about the relationship between events. Underline the verb that is in the wrong tense. Then write the correct verb.

1. Last weekend, Max finds an old diary in the attic and showed it to his mother. _____

2. The diary was dusty and they will wonder how old it was. _____

3. Max's mother reads the date on the first entry. She was so surprised, she almost dropped the diary on the floor. _____

4. Max couldn't believe the diary will belong to someone who lived in 1774. _____

5. "This diary was older than the U.S.!" he says, and his mother laughs. _____

> Revisit a piece of your writing. Edit the draft to make sure all tenses are used correctly.

Review Verb Tenses

Present Tense	Past Tense	Future Tense
The alien visits Earth. The author writes about aliens.	The alien visited Earth. The author wrote about aliens.	The alien will visit Earth. The author will write about aliens.

▸ **Write which tense of the verb in parentheses correctly completes the sentence. Then write the correct tense of the verb.**

1. The author (use) Pluto as the setting of his next book. _____

2. For his last book, the author (choose) Venus for the setting. _____

3. My brother (read) a chapter of his favorite science book every day. _____

4. He now (enjoy) reading stories about space travel. _____

5. Last year, he (like) books about dinosaurs. _____

6. I wonder what type of books he (like) next. _____

▸ **This paragraph contains four errors in verb tense. Underline each error. On the line below, correct the errors and tell which verb tense is correct.**

The famous science fiction author signed copies of her book later today at 4:00 p.m. I can't wait! Yesterday my mom tells me about the book signing. I finish reading the book last night. In the book, all the characters live on Earth, but Earth is very different. The characters' cars and computers are tiny. The characters can enlarge and shrink themselves to fit into their cars or use their computers. When I meet the author, I ask her if she really thinks we will be able to change our own size in the future.

7. _____   9. _____

8. _____   10. _____

Connect to Writing: Using the Correct Verb Tense

> **Read the selection and choose the best answer to each question.**

Chloe wrote a paragraph about a movie. Read her paragraph and look for any revisions she should make. Then answer the questions that follow.

The New Movie

(1) The movie begins when the boy's older brother joins the militia. (2) The firing cannons are so loud, I missed what the brother tells his captain. (3) The story gets exciting when the boy borrows a horse after he hurts his ankle. (4) When I leave the theater, I wanted to learn how to ride a horse. (5) I liked the movie so much that I tell my friends to see it.

1. What change, if any, should be made to Sentence 4?

    A. When I left the theater, I want to learn how to ride a horse.

    B. When I left the theater, I wanted to learn how to ride a horse.

    C. When I leave the theater, I wanted to learn how to rode a horse.

    D. Make no change.

2. What change, if any, should be made to Sentence 5?

    A. Change *tell* to *told*.

    B. Change *see* to *saw*.

    C. Change *friends* to *friend*.

    D. Make no change.

> **Have you seen a good movie lately? Write two or three sentences about it.**

_____

_____

_____

_____

Regular Verbs

> Most verbs are **regular verbs**. They form their past tense by adding *-ed*
> or *-d*. A regular verb also adds *-ed* when it is used with the helping verbs
> *has, have,* or *had.*
>
> **walk**, walked, have walked
> **live**, lived, has lived
>
> If a verb ends in a vowel followed by a consonant, double the consonant
> and add *-ed.* If a verb ends in a consonant followed by *y*, change the *y* to *i*
> and add *-ed.*
>
> **stop**, stopped, has stopped
> **cry**, cried, had cried

> **Write the past tense of each verb listed. Then write a sentence using the verb in the
> past tense.**

1. travel _____

   _____

2. beg _____

   _____

3. use _____

   _____

4. carry _____

   _____

5. injure _____

   _____

> **Revisit a piece of your writing. Edit the draft to make sure all regular verbs are used
> correctly.**

Grade 5 • Regular and Irregular Verbs

Irregular Verbs

Some verbs are **irregular**. These verbs don't add -ed or -d to form the past tense. Some very common verbs are irregular.

be: was/were	go: went	eat: ate	become: became
have: had	do: did	buy: bought	leave: left

> **Write the verbs and tell whether they are regular or irregular.**

1. Annie went to the library every weekend because she liked it there.

   _____

2. She spent her time reading stories about people who fought in the Revolution.

   _____

3. Sometimes hours passed before Annie stopped to check the time.

   _____

4. The librarian always smiled when Annie suddenly rushed out.

   _____

5. Annie's family ate at six o'clock and Annie always got home just before that.

   _____

> **Revisit a piece of your writing. Edit the draft to make sure all irregular verbs are used correctly.**

Past-Tense Forms of Irregular Verbs

For many **irregular verbs**, the form that is used with a helping verb is the same as the past tense. For others, it is different from the past tense.

Verb	Past Tense	With a Helping Verb
be	was (were)	has been
go	went	have gone
do	did	has done
know	knew	has known
ride	rode	have ridden

> Read the sentence and think about what form the irregular verbs should take. Underline the verb that is in the wrong form. Then write the correct verb form. Item 5 has more than one verb in the wrong form.

1. Samuel had went to take food to the soldiers. _____

2. His father had knew that he wanted to do it. _____

3. He been surprised that he had left to the house so early. _____

4. He had came downstairs to find him already gone. _____

5. However, Samuel had forgot the food money she had gave him. _____

> Revisit a piece of your writing. Edit the draft to make sure all past tenses of irregular verbs are used correctly.

Review Regular and Irregular Verbs

> **Irregular verbs** do not add -ed to form their past or past participle forms. It is a good idea to memorize the forms of each irregular verb.

> Fill in the missing form for each verb.

Present	Past	Past Participle
1. ring	rang	(have) _____
2. break	_____	(have) broken
3. swim	_____	(have) swum
4. take	_____	(have) taken
5. throw	threw	(have) _____
6. speak	spoke	(have) _____

> Circle the four errors in verb form in this paragraph. Write the correct form on the line.

He keeped a journal. He had told his nephew about it. The nephew read the journal. Then he wrote about his uncle's war experience. Many people boughten the book. They were surprised to learn what the war was like. They thinked the book was very interesting.

7. _____

8. _____

9. _____

10. _____

> Revisit a piece of your writing. Edit the draft to make sure all future-tense verbs are used correctly.

Connect to Writing: Using Regular and Irregular Verbs

> **Read the selection and choose the best answer to each question.**

John wrote a paragraph about a baseball game. Read his paragraph and look for any revisions he should make. Then answer the questions that follow.

An Exciting Game!

(1) I got to see my favorite team play a game at a huge stadium. (2) They have win more games than they've lost this season. (3) The game was exciting. (4) My favorite player hit a home run! (5) We eat popcorn and hot dogs during the seventh inning. (6) I can't wait to go back!

1. Sentence 2 contains an error. Which of the following is the best way to rewrite the sentence?

    A. They have win more games than they've lose this season.

    B. They have won more games than they've lost this season.

    C. They have win more games than they've loose this season.

    D. Make no change.

2. What change, if any, should be made to Sentence 5?

    A. Change *eat* to *ate*.

    B. Chang *during* to *daring*.

    C. Change *eat* to *eated*.

    D. Make no change.

> **Have you seen a sports event in person? Write two or three sentences about it.**

_____

_____

_____

_____

Verbs *Be* and *Have*

The verbs *be* and *have* are irregular verbs. They change forms when the subject changes. The subject and verb in a sentence must agree in number and tense.

singular subject and present-tense helping verb
She is looking out the window.
The weather **forecas**t has predicted rain.

plural subject and past-tense helping verb
They were wearing raincoats.
Gary and I had brought umbrellas.

> **Underline the correct helping verb in parentheses for each sentence.**

1. My mom and I (has, had) gone out for a walk.

2. The sun (were, is) shining brightly in the blue sky.

3. The thick clouds (are, is) moving quickly.

4. Large droplets of rain (had, is) fallen.

5. We (am, are) running into the house for shelter.

6. The wind (were, was) blowing outside.

7. I (are, am) not going outside until it stops raining.

8. The drenched cat (has, have) returned to the house.

9. The cat (has, is) tried to shake off the water from his fur.

10. I (am, have) found a towel to dry the cat's fur.

> **Revisit a piece of your writing. Edit the draft to make sure the verbs *be* and *have* are used correctly.**

Verb Phrases with *Be* and *Have*

A **verb phrase** contains more than one verb. The verbs *could, should, would,* or *must* are followed by another verb to form a verb phrase. The second verb in the verb phrase is often *be* or *have*.

> **verb phrase**
> It <u>could be</u> dangerous in the Wild West.
> I <u>would have brought</u> some granola for a snack.

> Read each sentence. Write *be* or *have* on the line to complete each verb phrase.

1. During the summer, the desert must _____ hot in the afternoon.

2. You should _____ plenty of water with you at all times.

3. If you feel dizzy, you could _____ suffering from the heat.

4. I would _____ worn a hat to protect myself from sunburn.

5. Look next to the tree where we _____ placed the picnic basket.

6. I will not _____ joining you at the movie tomorrow.

> Read each sentence. Choose the verb in parentheses that best fits the meaning of the sentence. Write the verb on the line.

7. (must/could) The children _____ have been tired after the long walk.

8. (would/should) Don't worry. I _____ be home before the thunderstorm hits.

9. (must/would) It _____ be helpful to know what the weather will be like tomorrow.

10. (should/must) The sun _____ be shining tomorrow, but you never know for sure!

> Revisit a piece of your writing. Edit the draft to make sure the verbs *be* and *have* are used correctly.

Consistent Verb Tenses

> When using the verbs *be* and *have*, remember to use verb tenses consistently. In order for your sentences to be correct, the verbs must be in the same tense.
>
> **Not correct**
> The students <u>had gone</u> on a field trip before, and they <u>had remember</u> how much fun they had.
>
> **Correct**
> The students <u>had gone</u> on a field trip before, and they <u>had remembered</u> how much fun they had.

> **Rewrite each sentence so that the verbs are in the same tense as the underlined verb phrase.**

1. A deer <u>had grazed</u> in the park before a noisy dog chase it away.

   _____

2. Heavy rain <u>had fallen</u> a few days earlier and floods the streets.

   _____

3. Mrs. Thomas <u>was looking</u> for a shady tree, and everyone is going to sit under it.

   _____

4. She <u>had supplied</u> snacks for everyone, and the students mix lemonade.

   _____

5. They <u>are going</u> to sing songs, and then they play games.

   _____

> **Revisit a piece of your writing. Edit the draft to make sure the verbs *be* and *have* are used correctly.**

Review the Verbs *Be* and *Have*

The chart below shows the present- and past-tense forms of *be* and *have*.

Subject	Form of *be* Present	Form of *be* Past	Form of *have* Present	Form of *have* Past
I	am	was	have	had
You (singular)	are	were	have	had
He, She, It, singular subject	is	was	has	had
You (plural)	are	were	have	had
We, They, plural subject	are	were	have	had

> **Write the form of *be* or *have* in parentheses that best completes each sentence.**

1. Polar bears (is, are) patient hunters. _____

2. Polar bear cubs (is, are) about the size of a rat when they are born. _____

3. The polar bear cub (has, have) been with its mother for nearly a year. _____

4. You should (has, have) seen how big the bear was! _____

5. Its sense of smell (is, are) very powerful. _____

6. The polar bear (has, have) eaten all of the meat. _____

7. They (is, are) protected from the cold by layers of blubber. _____

8. Polar bears (is, are) my favorite animal. _____

9. There (is, are) few animals with teeth as sharp as the polar bear. _____

10. The animal (is, are) found in some of the coldest regions. _____

> **Revisit a piece of your writing. Edit the draft to make sure the verbs *be* and *have* are used correctly.**

Connect to Writing: Using the Verbs *Be* and *Have*

> Read the selection and choose the best answer to each question.

Lucy wrote a paragraph about a storm. Read her paragraph and look for any revisions she should make. Then answer the questions that follow.

Boom!

(1) There was a clap of thunder outside. (2) The thunder be making my dog nervous. (3) I worried the power would go out. (4) Lightning lit up the dark sky. (5) I has flashlights in case the power went out. (6) But the storm ended quickly.

1. Sentence 2 contains an error. Which of the following is the best way to rewrite the sentence?

   A. The thunder nervous was my dog.

   B. The thunder was making my dog nervous.

   C. The thunder was made my dog nervous.

   D. Make no change.

2. What change, if any, should be made to Sentence 5?

   A. Change *I has flashlights* to *I flashlights have*.

   B. Change *I has flashlights* to *I had flashlights*.

   C. Change *power went* to *power had*.

   D. Make no change.

> Have you ever been caught in a bad storm? Write two or three sentences about it.

_____

_____

_____

_____

Perfect Tenses

The **present perfect tense** of a verb shows an action that began in the past and is still happening. To write the present perfect tense, use *has* or *have* as a helping verb. Then write the correct form of the main verb.

> **present perfect tense**
>
> She <u>has lived</u> in the village since she was born.
>
> They <u>have taken</u> this road many times.

> Write the present perfect tense of the verb in parentheses on the line.

1. Angel and I (know) _____ each other since third grade.

2. Chess (be) _____ a part of our culture for a long time.

3. We (play) _____ many games of chess together.

4. Jusef (learn) _____ to play chess, too.

5. A new family (move) _____ into town.

6. The new girl (tell) _____ us about traditions in her culture.

7. They (be) _____ busy unpacking their things.

8. I (finish) _____ all my extra chores.

9. We (be) _____ looking for him all day.

10. She (talk) _____ about how to find him.

> Revisit a piece of your writing. Edit the draft to make sure the perfect tenses are used correctly.

Past Perfect Tenses *Had*

The **past perfect tense** of a verb shows an action that happened before a certain time in the past. To write the past perfect tense, use *had* as a helping verb. Then write the correct form of the main verb.

> **past perfect tense**
> He <u>had wanted</u> to visit his friend on her birthday.
> We <u>had given</u> her flowers and a birthday cake before.

> **Write the past perfect tense of the verb in parentheses on the line.**

1. We (stop) _____ fishing when the lake froze over.

2. I already (eat) _____ by the time the guests came.

3. Before we knew it, they (leave) _____ the building for the ceremony.

4. She (help) _____ gather fruits and nuts.

5. He (read) _____ the old book that belonged to his grandmother.

6. Rudy never (see) _____ a bear before.

7. She (make) _____ a special blanket for the baby.

8. You (promise) _____ to walk through the woods with me.

9. They (try) _____ to bake a cake.

10. After dinner, we (decide) _____ to meet again next week.

> **Revisit a piece of your writing. Edit the draft to make sure the past perfect tenses are used correctly.**

Perfect Tenses *Will Have*

The **future perfect tense** of a verb shows an action that will be finished by a certain time in the future. To form the future perfect tense, write *will have* before the correct form of the main verb.

future perfect tense

I will have played ten games by the end of the season.

They will have driven across the country by next week.

> Write the future perfect tense of the verb in parentheses on the line.

1. By custom, we (finish) _____ our breakfast long before nine o'clock.

2. We (clean) _____ up by the time you get home.

3. Tanya (have) _____ enough time to make the cake for the festival.

4. By next June, Jordan (complete) _____ dance lessons.

5. If she reads every book on her list, Carmen (read) _____ ten books about ancient cultures.

6. Our class (earn) _____ enough for our trip by next week.

7. She (tell) _____ them the news about the festival before they read about it.

8. This horse (be) _____ groomed and ready to ride in the parade by noon.

9. I (sell) _____ the books over the weekend.

10. After the class, they (ask) _____ more questions than anyone.

> Revisit a piece of your writing. Edit the draft to make sure the future perfect tenses are used correctly.

Review Perfect Tenses

Add *has, have,* or *had* to the past-tense form of the verb to make the **perfect tense**. Irregular verbs have special forms to show the past.

Verb	Past Tense	Perfect Tense
have	had	(has, have, had) had
think	thought	(has, have, had) thought
say	said	(has, have, had) said

▶ Rewrite each sentence, changing the underlined verb to a form of the perfect tense.

1. Rosa <u>bring</u> her camera to the cliff.

_____

2. Ruben <u>say</u> he could solve any mystery.

_____

3. They <u>go</u> on this museum tour earlier in the year.

_____

4. Ruben <u>looked</u> closely at all of the exhibits.

_____

5. We <u>investigated</u> other mysteries.

_____

▶ Revisit a piece of your writing. Edit the draft to make sure the perfect tenses are used correctly.

_____

Connect to Writing: Using Perfect Tenses

> **Read the selection and choose the best answer to each question.**

Maia wrote a paragraph about adopting a kitten. Read her paragraph and look for any revisions she should make. Then answer the questions that follow.

My New Kitten

(1) I had gone to the pet store to pick out a new pet. (2) I picked out a kitten with white paws. (3) The kitten had a meow that sounded like a squeak. (4) By this time next year, the kitten will grow. (5) Right now she is tiny and very playful.

1. Which of the following is the best way to rewrite Sentence 3?

   A. The kitten had meowed that sounded like a squeak.

   B. The kitten had a meow that had sounding like a squeak.

   C. The kitten had a meow that have sounded like a squeak.

   D. Make no change.

2. What change, if any, should be made to Sentence 4?

   A. Change *will grow* to *will have grown*.

   B. Change *will* to *have*.

   C. Change *grow* to *grown*.

   D. Make no change.

> **What pet would you like to adopt? Write two or three sentences about it.**

_____

_____

_____

_____

Easily Confused Verbs

Some verbs are easily confused because their meanings are closely related. Study the meanings of these easily confused verbs to avoid using the wrong one.

sit: to lower yourself on to a seat
set: to place an item on to something

can: able to do
may: allowed to do

teach: to give instruction to someone
learn: to receive instruction from someone

lie: to recline on something
lay: to put an item on top of something

rise: to get up or to stand up
raise: to lift something up

I'm going to <u>sit</u> in the shade under a tree.
She <u>set</u> the diary down on the bed.

▶ **Underline the correct verb in each sentence below.**

1. Natalie is (teaching/learning) how to use a lasso.

2. The smoke was (rising/raising) from the valley below.

3. The cowboy was ready to (lie/lay) down his rope at the end of the day.

4. She (sit/set) her poncho on the ground.

5. I (may/can) be able to visit the ranch tomorrow.

▶ **Revisit a piece of your writing. Edit the draft to make sure easily confused words are used correctly.**

Identify Easily Confused Verbs

Study the meanings of each of these words to avoid using the wrong one. Pay attention to the part of speech of each.

good (adj.) favorable, useful
well (adj.) healthy
well (adv.) with skill, properly
their (pron.) possessive of *they*
there (adj.) location
they're contraction of *they* are

> Conditions are <u>good</u> for riding outdoors.
> The soldier fought <u>well</u> after eating a good meal.

> **Underline the word in parentheses that correctly completes each sentence.**

1. You had to be a (good, well) horseback rider to be a vaquero.

2. It was difficult to hear (good, well) because of the howling coyotes.

3. He didn't feel (good, well) after eating his breakfast.

4. Luckily, (there, their, they're) ranch was not in the path of the wild fire.

5. The ranch was the largest in the area, and many cowboys worked (there, their, they're).

> **Revisit a piece of your writing. Edit the draft to make sure easily confused words are used correctly.**

Choosing the Right Word

To help you choose the correct word for a situation, try saying the sentence aloud. Memorize the meanings of easily confused words that sound alike. You can also check definitions in a dictionary.

affect (v.) to influence or cause a change
effect (n.) a result
few (adj.) small in number
less (adj.) small in amount

> The fog will <u>affect</u> their ability to see the enemy.
> The fog had no <u>effect</u> on their spirits, however.

> **Underline the word in parentheses that best completes each sentence.**

1. (There, Their, They're) are a lot of books in the library about the Mexican-American War.

2. I found a book about the famous battles and (sit, set) it on the counter.

3. The librarian told us that each student (may, can) take out two books about the Gold Rush.

4. This rule will (affect, effect) which books I decide to take home.

5. This library has (few, less) biographies of cowboys.

> **Revisit a piece of your writing. Edit the draft to make sure easily confused words are used correctly.**

Review Easily Confused Verbs

Some pairs of verbs have such closely related meanings that they are easily confused. Most of these verbs are **irregular verbs**. A few are **helping verbs**. By studying the meanings of both verbs, you can avoid using the wrong one in your speaking and writing.

can: able to do

sit: to lower yourself on to a seat

teach: to give instruction to someone

lie: to recline on something

rise: to get up or to stand up

may: allowed to do

set: to place an item on to something

learn: to receive instruction from someone

lay: to put an item on top of something

raise: to lift something up

> **Underline the correct verb in each sentence below.**

1. The cat (sits, sets) on the chair.

2. You (can, may) go to the concert.

3. The cat (rises, raises) off the chair.

4. The teacher (teaches, learns) us how to solve math problems.

5. The cat (lays, lies) on the floor.

> **Revisit a piece of your writing. Edit the draft to make sure easily confused words are used correctly.**

Connect to Writing: Using Verbs Correctly

> **Read the selection and choose the best answer to each question.**

Stacey wrote a paragraph about the rodeo. Read her paragraph and look for any revisions she should make. Then answer the questions that follow.

The Rodeo

(1) Rodeos are entertainment for millions of people. (2) They're also a well way to keep the traditions of vaqueros and cowboys alive. (3) There are many sports in a rodeo, and each of them reflects the jobs that cowboys performed well for generations. (4) For example, in a steer roping event, a cowboy sitting on a horse, raises a lasso and throws it at just the right moment to rope the steer. (5) Many years ago, cowboys on the range used the same skills to round up cattle. (6) Now there are fewer cowboys than there once were. (7) But rodeos carry on there traditions. (8) The effect is that cowboy culture lives on.

1. Sentence 2 contains an error. Which of the following is the best way to rewrite the sentence?

    A. Their also a well way to keep the traditions of vaqueros and cowboys alive.

    B. They're also a good way to keep the traditions of vaqueros and cowboys alive.

    C. There also a well way to keep the traditions of vaqueros and cowboys alive.

    D. Make no change.

2. What change, if any, should be made to Sentence 7?

    A. Change *there* to *they're*.

    B. Chang *carry* to *curry*.

    C. Change *there* to *their*.

    D. Make no change.

> **Have you ever ridden a horse? Would you like to? Write two or three sentences about it.**

_____

_____

_____

Adjectives

An **adjective** is a word that describes a noun or a pronoun. It tells *what kind* or *how many*. Adjectives that tell us *what kind* are called **descriptive adjectives**. Capitalize a descriptive adjective that gives the origin of the person, place, or thing being described.

what kind	Emily enjoys <u>suspense</u> stories.
origin	Kimberly likes to read <u>Japanese</u> comics called manga.
how many	The <u>three</u> girls share their books.

▶ **Underline the adjective or adjectives in each sentence. For each adjective, write *what kind, origin*, or *how many* to show the kind of information given.**

1. The hero in this adventure story is named Gregory. _____

2. He carries a tiny computer with him. _____

3. His jacket has pictures of Chinese warriors! _____

4. Gregory flies an invisible American spaceship. _____

5. Did you ever write a story about a comic-book hero? _____

6. I tried to write one about a brainy girl two years ago. _____

7. I could never draw the right images to tell the story. _____

8. Someday I'll start again and find a good, exciting idea for a story. _____

9. He went to the restaurant to order some Italian food. _____

10. We heard all about her excellent grades. _____

▶ **Revisit a piece of your writing. Edit the draft to make sure adjectives are used correctly.**

Adjectives and Linking Verbs

An **adjective** does not always come before the noun or pronoun it describes. An adjective can also follow a linking verb, such as any form of *be. Smell, feel, taste, look,* and *sound* can also be linking verbs.

> **subject + linking verb + adjective**
> Linda is <u>talented</u> at art.
> Oscar feels <u>tired</u> of drawing.
> The new book looks <u>wonderful</u>.

> ▶ **For each sentence, circle the adjective that follows the linking verb. Then underline the noun or pronoun that the adjective describes.**

1. Sarah is excited about creating illustrations to help tell the story in her comic book.

2. After leaving his favorite comic in the rain, Leo felt unhappy.

3. Harry felt lucky because he got the last illustrated copy in the store.

4. The macaroni and cheese tasted delicious and gave me the energy to keep drawing.

5. In my first draft, the battle seems boring.

> ▶ **Revisit a piece of your writing. Edit the draft to make sure adjectives and linking verbs are used correctly.**

Articles

The words *the*, *a*, and *an* are adjectives called **articles**. *The* is a **definite article** because it points out a specific person, place, or thing. *A* and *an* are **indefinite articles** because they refer to any person, place, or thing. Use *an* before a noun that begins with a vowel sound.

A newspaper launched a new cartoon strip. The paper is a small, hometown paper. An edition of the newspaper comes out every day.

> **Write the correct articles to fill in the blanks. Reread all the sentences to be sure they make sense.**

1. Before creating _____ new comic book, you have to come up with _____ idea.

2. It is also helpful if you are _____ artist who can bring characters to life.

3. Perhaps you want _____ book to be about _____ awesome hero.

4. _____ hero has _____ series of adventures.

5. Each illustration can show _____ good quality _____ hero has.

6. Of course, _____ hero wins _____ conflicts.

7. Finally, _____ villains are vanquished.

8. _____ book comes to _____ end.

9. The movie was written based on _____ story in _____ book.

10. We watched _____ movie with _____ tub of popcorn.

> **Revisit a piece of your writing. Edit the draft to make sure articles are used correctly.**

Review Adjectives and Articles

An **adjective** describes a noun or a pronoun. It tells *what kind* or *how many*. It also can give the origin of a person, place, or thing.

An adjective can follow a linking verb.

A, *an*, and *the* are special adjectives called **articles**. *A* and *an* refer to any noun. *The* refers to a specific noun.

> Underline the descriptive adjective in each sentence. Circle the noun or pronoun the adjective describes.

1. I am excited to read the menu.

2. We ate at the Vietnamese restaurant.

3. They ordered three entrees.

4. The food on the plate in front of me smelled spicy.

5. My generous friend paid for our dinner.

> Write the correct article in parentheses to complete each sentence.

6. A mammoth is (a, an) extinct elephant from long ago. _____

7. Jorge visited (the, an) Natural History Museum. _____

8. Those fossils are the oldest in (a, the) museum. _____

9. I wrote (an, a) essay about dinosaurs. _____

10. I read (a, an) book about this museum's history. _____

> Revisit a piece of your writing. Edit the draft to make sure adjectives and articles are used correctly.

Grade 5 • Adjectives

Connect to Writing: Using Adjectives and Articles

> Read the selection and choose the best answer to each question.

Lola wrote a paragraph about comic strips. Read her paragraph and look for any revisions she should make. Then answer the questions that follow.

A New Comic Strip

(1) Harry drew an action-packed comic strip based on a movie. (2) His main character was an archaeologist. (3) The archaeologist figured out the code to open a pyramid. (4) He saw piles of treasure inside the tomb. (5) He fought off the murderous, violent thieves who wanted the priceless treasure.

1. Which of the following is the best way to rewrite Sentence 2 to add more adjectives?

   A. His main character was an archaeologist and a teacher.

   B. His main character was a daring, brilliant archaeologist.

   C. His main character was the archaeologist.

   D. Make no change.

2. What change, if any, could be made to Sentence 4 to add more adjectives?

   A. Add *glittering* to describe *piles*.

   B. Add *golden* to describe *treasure*.

   C. Add *gloomy* to describe *tomb*.

   D. All of the above.

> What is your favorite movie? Write two or three sentences about it.

_____

_____

_____

_____

Adverbs That Tell *How, Where, When, How Often*

An **adverb** is a word that usually describes a verb. Adverbs tell *how, when,* or *where* an action happens. Many adverbs end with *-ly*.

> **how:** They played the music <u>loudly</u>.
> **when:** He came <u>early</u>.
> **where:** He went <u>inside</u>.
> **how often:** I <u>always</u> bring my lunch to school.

> Underline the adverb in each sentence. Write whether the adverb tells *ho ~* *where,* or *how often*.

1. Nola jumped ahead in the pages to look for the answer. _____

2. She eagerly worked on the design for her project. _____

3. Nola finally found the solution to her problem. _____

4. She had never achieved such an honor. _____

5. Nola dreamily imagined her parents congratulating her. _____

> Revisit a piece of your writing. Edit the draft to make sure adverbs that ▬ *where,* and *how often* are used correctly.

Connect to Writing: Using Adjectives and Articles

> Read the selection and choose the best answer to each question.

Lola wrote a paragraph about comic strips. Read her paragraph and look for any revisions she should make. Then answer the questions that follow.

A New Comic Strip

(1) Harry drew an action-packed comic strip based on a movie. (2) His main character was an archaeologist. (3) The archaeologist figured out the code to open a pyramid. (4) He saw piles of treasure inside the tomb. (5) He fought off the murderous, violent thieves who wanted the priceless treasure.

1. Which of the following is the best way to rewrite Sentence 2 to add more adjectives?

   A. His main character was an archaeologist and a teacher.

   B. His main character was a daring, brilliant archaeologist.

   C. His main character was the archaeologist.

   D. Make no change.

2. What change, if any, could be made to Sentence 4 to add more adjectives?

   A. Add *glittering* to describe *piles*.

   B. Add *golden* to describe *treasure*.

   C. Add *gloomy* to describe *tomb*.

   D. All of the above.

> What is your favorite movie? Write two or three sentences about it.

_____

_____

_____

_____

Name _____

Adverbs That Tell *How, Where, When, How Often*

An **adverb** is a word that usually describes a verb. Adverbs tell *how, when,* or *where* an action happens. Many adverbs end with *-ly.*

> **how:** They played the music <u>loudly</u>.
> **when:** He came <u>early</u>.
> **where:** He went <u>inside</u>.
> **how often:** I <u>always</u> bring my lunch to school.

▶ **Underline the adverb in each sentence. Write whether the adverb tells *how,* wr** **where,** or *how often.*

1. Nola jumped ahead in the pages to look for the answer. _____

2. She eagerly worked on the design for her project. _____

3. Nola finally found the solution to her problem. _____

4. She had never achieved such an honor. _____

5. Nola dreamily imagined her parents congratulating her. _____

▶ **Revisit a piece of your writing. Edit the draft to make sure adverbs that tell *h*** **where,** and *how often* are used correctly.

Connect to Writing: Using Adjectives and Articles

▷ **Read the selection and choose the best answer to each question.**

Lola wrote a paragraph about comic strips. Read her paragraph and look for any revisions she should make. Then answer the questions that follow.

A New Comic Strip

(1) Harry drew an action-packed comic strip based on a movie. (2) His main character was an archaeologist. (3) The archaeologist figured out the code to open a pyramid. (4) He saw piles of treasure inside the tomb. (5) He fought off the murderous, violent thieves who wanted the priceless treasure.

1. Which of the following is the best way to rewrite Sentence 2 to add more adjectives?

   A. His main character was an archaeologist and a teacher.
   B. His main character was a daring, brilliant archaeologist.
   C. His main character was the archaeologist.
   D. Make no change.

2. What change, if any, could be made to Sentence 4 to add more adjectives?

   A. Add *glittering* to describe *piles*.
   B. Add *golden* to describe *treasure*.
   C. Add *gloomy* to describe *tomb*.
   D. All of the above.

▷ **What is your favorite movie? Write two or three sentences about it.**

_____
_____
_____
_____

Name _____

Adverbs That Tell *How, Where, When, How Often*

An **adverb** is a word that usually describes a verb. Adverbs tell *how, when,* or *where* an action happens. Many adverbs end with *-ly*.

> **how:** They played the music <u>loudly</u>.
> **when:** He came <u>early</u>.
> **where:** He went <u>inside</u>.
> **how often:** I <u>always</u> bring my lunch to school.

> Underline the adverb in each sentence. Write whether the adverb tells *how,* ~~when~~, *where,* or *how often.*

1. Nola jumped ahead in the pages to look for the answer. _____

2. She eagerly worked on the design for her project. _____

3. Nola finally found the solution to her problem. _____

4. She had never achieved such an honor. _____

5. Nola dreamily imagined her parents congratulating her. _____

> Revisit a piece of your writing. Edit the draft to make sure adverbs that tell *how,* ~~when~~, *where,* and *how often* are used correctly.